# THE WORLD ALMANAC™

# 2023 CALENDAR

## A YEAR OF FASCINATING FACTS

Andrews McMeel
PUBLISHING®

D0998622

www.andrewsmcmeel.com

www.andrewsmcmeel.com

ISBN: 978-1-5248-7318-9

Start dates for the seasons of the year are presented in Universal Time.

Every effort has been made to ensure the accuracy of listed holiday dates; however, some may have changed after publication for official or cultural reasons.

## THIS WEEK IN CELEBRITY BIRTHDAYS:

**12/31** ...... Diane von Fürstenberg (1946– )

**1/1** ........... Grandmaster Flash (1958– )

**1/2** .......... Isaac Asimov (1920–1992)

**1/3** .......... Michael Schumacher (1969– )

**1/4** .......... Kris Bryant (1992– )

**1/5** .......... Bradley Cooper (1975– )

**1/6** .......... Kate McKinnon (1984– )

# 31/1

**SAT/SUN**
**DEC/JAN**
**2022/2023**

/New Year's Day
/Kwanzaa ends (USA)

# THE WORLD ALMANAC

## TODAY IN SPORTS HISTORY

In 1984, Miami upset heavily favored Nebraska in the Orange Bowl, 31–30, as Nebraska failed on a two-point conversion at game's end.

**2**

**MONDAY**
**JANUARY**
**2023**

New Year's Day (observed) (NZ, Australia, UK)

# THE WORLD ALMANAC

**TODAY IN HISTORY**

In 1977, Apple was incorporated by co-founders Steve Jobs and Steve Wozniak.

**3**

**TUESDAY
JANUARY
2023**

Bank Holiday (UK–Scotland)

## THE WORLD ALMANAC

**BY THE NUMBERS**

The International Space Station has a mass of 924,739 pounds and is about as long as a football field with a length of 357.5 feet.

### THE WORLD ALMANAC

**TODAY IN HISTORY**

In 1914, Ford Motor Company announced it was raising basic wages from $2.34 for a nine-hour workday to $5 for an eight-hour workday.

**5**

# THE WORLD ALMANAC

The Anthropocene is a proposed epoch of geologic time marked by a significant influence of human activity on the environment. Suggested starting points include the mid-twentieth century (when extensive testing of nuclear and thermonuclear bombs began) and the Industrial Revolution of the nineteenth century.

**6**

**FRIDAY**
**JANUARY**
**2023**

## THIS WEEK IN CELEBRITY BIRTHDAYS:

**7** .............. Katie Couric (1957– )

**8** .............. Stephen Hawking (1942–2018)

**9** .............. Dave Matthews (1967– )

**10** ........... George Foreman (1949– )

**11** ........... Mary J. Blige (1971– )

**12** ........... Jeff Bezos (1964– )

**13** ........... Julia Louis-Dreyfus (1961– )

# 7/8

**TODAY IN SPORTS HISTORY**

In 2013, results of the annual Baseball Hall of Fame ballot were announced. For the first time since 1996, no new living members were elected.

**9**

## THE WORLD ALMANAC

**TODAY IN HISTORY**

In 1927, the landmark Fritz Lang film *Metropolis* was first released in Germany.

**10**

### THE WORLD ALMANAC

**BY THE NUMBERS**

An estimated 25 million cloud-to-ground lightning bolts happen in the U.S. each year. They killed an annual average of thirty-nine people in 1990–2020.

**11**

# THE WORLD ALMANAC

**TODAY IN HISTORY**

In 1967, psychology professor James Bedford died. He became the first person to be intentionally cryopreserved after death.

**12**

**THURSDAY
JANUARY
2023**

## Tallest Mountains in the Alps

| Peak, country | Height (feet) |
| --- | --- |
| Mont Blanc, France–Italy | 15,781 |
| Dufourspitze (highest of Monte Rosa group), Switzerland | 15,203 |
| Dom, Switzerland | 14,911 |
| Liskamm, Italy–Switzerland | 14,852 |
| Weisshorn, Switzerland | 14,780 |

**13**

**FRIDAY**
**JANUARY**
**2023**

# THE WORLD ALMANAC

## THIS WEEK IN CELEBRITY BIRTHDAYS:

**14** ........... LL Cool J (1968– )

**15** ........... Martin Luther King Jr. (1929–1968)

**16** ........... Lin-Manuel Miranda (1980– )

**17** ........... Betty White (1922–2021)

**18** ........... A. A. Milne (1882–1956)

**19** ........... Dolly Parton (1946– )

**20** ........... Buzz Aldrin (1930– )

# 14/15

**SAT/SUN**
**JANUARY**
**2023**

**TODAY IN SPORTS HISTORY**

In 1961, Mickey Mantle signed a contract for an annual salary of $75,000, making him the highest-paid player in the American League.

## 16

**MONDAY**
**JANUARY**
**2023**

Martin Luther King Jr. Day (USA)

## THE WORLD ALMANAC

**TODAY IN HISTORY**

In 1991, a U.S.-led coalition launched airstrikes at targets in Kuwait and Iraq, marking the beginning of the Persian Gulf War.

**17**

**TUESDAY**
**JANUARY**
**2023**

**THE WORLD ALMANAC**

## BY THE NUMBERS

In the 1899–1900 school year, the average annual salary of an American public-school teacher was $325.

**18** | **WEDNESDAY**
**JANUARY**
**2023**

## TODAY IN HISTORY

In 1977, snow fell in Miami, Florida, for the first time in recorded history.

**19**

# THE WORLD ALMANAC

Of the five Great Lakes, only Lake Michigan is wholly in the U.S.;
the other lakes are shared with Canada.

**20**

# THE WORLD ALMANAC

## THIS WEEK IN CELEBRITY BIRTHDAYS:

**21** ............ Jack Nicklaus (1940– )

**22** ............ Guy Fieri (1968– )

**23** ............ Chita Rivera (1933– )

**24** ............ Edith Wharton (1862–1937)

**25** ............ Alicia Keys (1981– )

**26** ............ Ellen DeGeneres (1958– )

**27** ............ Alan Cumming (1965– )

# 21/22

**SAT/SUN**
**JANUARY**
**2023**

/Lunar New Year
(Year of the Rabbit)

# THE WORLD ALMANAC

## TODAY IN SPORTS HISTORY

In 1944, the Detroit Red Wings set a new record for the most one-sided hockey game by beating the New York Rangers 15–0.

**23**

**TODAY IN HISTORY**

In 1995, the O. J. Simpson murder trial began as the prosecution made its opening statement.

**24**

# THE WORLD ALMANAC

## BY THE NUMBERS

A Woods Hole Oceanographic Institution study published in 2010 calculated a mean depth of 12,081 feet for the world's oceans.

**25** | **WEDNESDAY**
**JANUARY**
**2023**

## THE WORLD ALMANAC

**TODAY IN HISTORY**

In 1950, the Indian constitution went into effect, marking the birth of the Republic of India.

**26**

Australia Day

# THE WORLD ALMANAC

Some common (and uncommon) names for animal collectives/groups:

- **grasshoppers:** cloud
- **hawks:** cast, kettle
- **hedgehogs:** array, prickle
- **hippopotamuses:** bloat
- **horses:** pair, team
- **hounds:** cry, mute, pack
- **hyenas:** cackle

**27**

**THE WORLD ALMANAC**

## THIS WEEK IN CELEBRITY BIRTHDAYS:

**1/28** ........ Jackson Pollock (1912–1956)

**1/29** ........ Oprah Winfrey (1954– )

**1/30** ........ Franklin D. Roosevelt (1882–1945)

**1/31** ........ Justin Timberlake (1981– )

**2/1** .......... Harry Styles (1994– )

**2/2** .......... Ayn Rand (1905–1982)

**2/3** .......... Norman Rockwell (1894–1978)

# 28/29

**SAT/SUN
JANUARY
2023**

# THE WORLD ALMANAC

**TODAY IN SPORTS HISTORY**

In 2002, Karl Malone became the second NBA player
(after Kareem Abdul-Jabbar) to score 34,000 career points.

**30** | **MONDAY**
**JANUARY**
**2023**

## THE WORLD ALMANAC

**TODAY IN HISTORY**

In 1606, Guy Fawkes was executed for his role in the Gunpowder Plot in Britain.

# THE WORLD ALMANAC

## BY THE NUMBERS

The transfer of charges in lightning generates a huge amount of heat, sending the temperature in the channel to 50,000°F or more and causing the air within it to expand rapidly. The sound of that expansion is thunder.

**1**

**WEDNESDAY**
**FEBRUARY**
**2023**

## THE WORLD ALMANAC

**TODAY IN HISTORY**

In 1922, James Joyce's masterwork *Ulysses* was first published in Paris.

**2**

# THE WORLD ALMANAC

Jimmy Carter (born October 1, 1924, in Plains, Georgia) was the first U.S. president to have been born in a hospital.

## THE WORLD ALMANAC

### THIS WEEK IN CELEBRITY BIRTHDAYS:

4 .............. Rosa Parks (1913–2005)

5 .............. Hank Aaron (1934–2021)

6 .............. Babe Ruth (1895–1948)

7 .............. Garth Brooks (1962– )

8 .............. Mary Steenburgen (1953– )

9 .............. Michael B. Jordan (1987– )

10 ............ Yara Shahidi (2000– )

**4/5**

SAT/SUN
**FEBRUARY**
2023

## THE WORLD ALMANAC

**TODAY IN HISTORY**

In 1918, the British Parliament's Representation of the People Act gave some women thirty years of age or older the right to vote for the first time.

**6**

**MONDAY**
**FEBRUARY**
**2023**

St. Brigid's Day (Ireland)
Waitangi Day (NZ)

THE WORLD ALMANAC

## TODAY IN SPORTS HISTORY

In 1976, the men's basketball teams for Purdue and Wisconsin both had perfect free-throw percentages—making a combined 47 of 47 from the line—as they faced each other in a regular season game.

**7**

**TUESDAY**
**FEBRUARY**
**2023**

## THE WORLD ALMANAC

**BY THE NUMBERS**

Since the U.S. Supreme Court was established in 1789 through the 2020–21 term, 115 justices have served on the court for an average of sixteen years each.

**8**

**TODAY IN HISTORY**

In 1971, legendary pitcher Satchel Paige became the first former Negro League player to be selected for induction into the Baseball Hall of Fame.

**9**

**THURSDAY**
**FEBRUARY**
**2023**

# THE WORLD ALMANAC

## Most Popular Cat Breeds

(According to The Cat Fanciers' Association's total registrations)

1. Ragdoll
2. Exotic
3. Maine Coon
4. Persian
5. British Shorthair

**10** | **FRIDAY**
**FEBRUARY**
**2023**

# THE WORLD ALMANAC

## THIS WEEK IN CELEBRITY BIRTHDAYS:

**11** ............ Jennifer Aniston (1969– )

**12** ............ Abraham Lincoln (1809–1865)

**13** ............ Mike Krzyzewski (1947– )

**14** ............ Renée Fleming (1959– )

**15** ............ Matt Groening (1954– )

**16** ............ Mahershala Ali (1974– )

**17** ............ Ed Sheeran (1991– )

**11/12**

SAT/SUN
**FEBRUARY**
**2023**

## THE WORLD ALMANAC

**TODAY IN HISTORY**

In 1945, Allied aircraft began bombing the German city of Dresden.

**13**

## THE WORLD ALMANAC

**TODAY IN SPORTS HISTORY**

In 1988, Bobby Allison became the oldest driver (age 50) to win the Daytona 500, while his son Davey Allison finished second. It was the race's first one-two father-son finish.

**14**

**TUESDAY**
**FEBRUARY**
**2023**

St. Valentine's Day

## BY THE NUMBERS

The first U.S. census, conducted in 1790, actually collected data over eighteen months, at a cost of about $44,000, or $1.2 million in current dollars.

## THE WORLD ALMANAC

---

**TODAY IN HISTORY**

In 1923, archaeologists unsealed the burial chamber of the recently rediscovered tomb of King Tutankhamun.

**16**

The following U.S. presidents were left-handed: James Garfield, Herbert Hoover, Harry S. Truman, Gerald Ford, Ronald Reagan, George H. W. Bush, Bill Clinton, and Barack Obama. (It is very possible that some presidents preceding Garfield were also left-handed but were trained to write right-handed.)

**17**

FRIDAY
**FEBRUARY**
2023

# THE WORLD ALMANAC

## THIS WEEK IN CELEBRITY BIRTHDAYS:

**18** ........... Toni Morrison (1931–2019)

**19** ........... Roger Goodell (1959– )

**20** ........... Olivia Rodrigo (2003– )

**21** ........... John Lewis (1940–2020)

**22** ........... Drew Barrymore (1975– )

**23** ........... W. E. B. Du Bois (1868–1963)

**24** ........... Floyd Mayweather Jr. (1977– )

# 18/19

**SAT/SUN**
**FEBRUARY**
**2023**

# THE WORLD ALMANAC

## TODAY IN HISTORY

In 1872, the Metropolitan Museum of Art opened to the public in New York City.

**20**

**MONDAY**
**FEBRUARY**
**2023**

Presidents' Day (USA)

# THE WORLD ALMANAC

## TODAY IN SPORTS HISTORY

In 1948, the National Association for Stock Car Auto Racing—now known as NASCAR—was incorporated.

**21**

**BY THE NUMBERS**

Ash Wednesday always occurs forty-six days before Easter.

**22**

Ash Wednesday

**THE WORLD ALMANAC**

### TODAY IN HISTORY

In 1945, Marines were photographed raising the U.S. flag on Iwo Jima.

**23**

**THURSDAY
FEBRUARY
2023**

# THE WORLD ALMANAC

## Most Densely Populated Countries
### (2021)

| Rank | Country | Persons per sq mi | Persons per sq km |
|------|---------|-------------------|-------------------|
| 1. | Monaco | 40,433.6 | 15,611.5 |
| 2. | Singapore | 21,429.1 | 8,273.8 |
| 3. | Vatican City* | 5,886.3 | 2,272.7 |
| 4. | Bahrain | 5,203.6 | 2,009.1 |
| 5. | Malta | 3,777.5 | 1,458.5 |

* = Population as of 2019.

**24**

**FRIDAY**
**FEBRUARY**
**2023**

## THE WORLD ALMANAC

**THIS WEEK IN CELEBRITY BIRTHDAYS:**

**2/25** ........ Rashida Jones (1976– )

**2/26** ........ Johnny Cash (1932–2003)

**2/27** ........ John Steinbeck (1902–1968)

**2/28** ........ John Turturro (1957– )

**3/1** .......... Justin Bieber (1994– )

**3/2** .......... Daniel Craig (1968– )

**3/3** .......... Jackie Joyner-Kersee (1962– )

# 25/26

**SAT/SUN**
**FEBRUARY**
**2023**

**TODAY IN HISTORY**

In 1973, American Indian Movement activists occupied the town of Wounded Knee on Pine Ridge Indian Reservation in South Dakota, beginning a standoff with federal marshals that lasted until May 8.

**27**

**TODAY IN SPORTS HISTORY**

In 1960, the U.S. men's hockey team defeated Czechoslovakia, 9–4, to win their first Olympic gold medal.

**28** | **TUESDAY**
**FEBRUARY**
**2023**

**BY THE NUMBERS**

Hells Canyon, through which the Snake River flows, is the deepest gorge in the United States, at 7,913 feet deep.

**1**

**WEDNESDAY**
**MARCH**
**2023**

St. David's Day (UK)

**THE WORLD ALMANAC**

### TODAY IN HISTORY

In 1933, the film *King Kong* premiered in New York.

**2**

**THURSDAY**
**MARCH**
**2023**

## Most Visited Sites in the National Park System
### (2020)

| Rank | Site (location) | Visits |
|------|-----------------|--------|
| 1. | Blue Ridge Parkway (North Carolina–Virginia) | 14,099,485 |
| 2. | Golden Gate National Recreation Area (California) | 12,400,045 |
| 3. | Great Smoky Mountains National Park (North Carolina–Tennessee) | 12,095,720 |
| 4. | Gateway National Recreation Area (New Jersey–New York) | 8,404,728 |
| 5. | Lake Mead National Recreation Area (Arizona–Nevada) | 8,016,510 |

**3** | **FRIDAY**
**MARCH**
**2023**

## THIS WEEK IN CELEBRITY BIRTHDAYS:

**4** .............. Catherine O'Hara (1954– )

**5** .............. Joel Osteen (1963– )

**6** .............. Michelangelo (1475–1564)

**7** .............. Jenna Fischer (1974– )

**8** .............. Lester Holt (1959– )

**9** .............. Oscar Isaac (1979– )

**10** ........... Carrie Underwood (1983– )

**4/5**

**SAT/SUN**
**MARCH**
**2023**

**THE WORLD ALMANAC**

### TODAY IN HISTORY

In 1943, Norman Rockwell's *Freedom from Want* painting was first published in *The Saturday Evening Post* magazine.

**6**

**MONDAY**
**MARCH**
**2023**

Purim (begins at sundown)
Labour Day (Australia—WA)

**THE WORLD ALMANAC**

### TODAY IN SPORTS HISTORY

In 1996, Magic Johnson became the second player in NBA history to reach 10,000 career assists.

**7**

**TUESDAY**
**MARCH**
**2023**

# THE WORLD ALMANAC

**BY THE NUMBERS**

Including the time zones of its overseas territories, France has twelve time zones—more than any other country in the world. Russia and the U.S. follow with eleven each.

**8**

International Women's Day

## THE WORLD ALMANAC

**TODAY IN HISTORY**

In 1959, Mattel introduced the Barbie doll at the American International Toy Fair in New York City.

**9**

**THURSDAY
MARCH
2023**

## Tallest Mountains in Antarctica

| Peak | Height (feet) |
| --- | --- |
| Vinson Massif | 16,066 |
| Tyree | 15,919 |
| Shinn | 15,750 |
| Gardner | 15,375 |
| Epperly | 15,100 |

**THE WORLD ALMANAC**

## THIS WEEK IN CELEBRITY BIRTHDAYS:

**11** ............ Anthony Davis (1993– )

**12** ............ Jack Kerouac (1922–1969)

**13** ............ Common (1972– )

**14** ............ Simone Biles (1997– )

**15** ............ Eva Longoria (1975– )

**16** ............ James Madison (1751–1836)

**17** ............ John Boyega (1992– )

# 11/12

**SAT/SUN**
**MARCH**
**2023**

/Daylight Saving Time begins
(USA, Canada)

# THE WORLD ALMANAC

## TODAY IN HISTORY

In 2013, the College of Cardinals selected Argentinean Jorge Mario Bergoglio as the Roman Catholic Church's first leader of Latin American origin. He took the name Pope Francis.

**13**

**MONDAY**
**MARCH**
**2023**

Eight Hours Day (Australia—TAS)
Labour Day (Australia—VIC)
Commonwealth Day (Australia, Canada, NZ, UK)

## THE WORLD ALMANAC

**TODAY IN SPORTS HISTORY**

In 1967, the AFL and NFL held their first common draft of college players.

## BY THE NUMBERS

At 5 feet, 4 inches tall, James Madison was the shortest person ever to serve as president of the United States. The tallest president was Abraham Lincoln, who was a full foot taller than Madison.

**15** WEDNESDAY
**MARCH**
**2023**

## THE WORLD ALMANAC

**TODAY IN HISTORY**

In 1802, President Thomas Jefferson signed legislation that established the U.S. Military Academy at West Point.

**16**

**THURSDAY**
**MARCH**
**2023**

There are twenty-eight counties in Ireland and six counties in Northern Ireland.

**17**

**FRIDAY**
**MARCH**
**2023**

St. Patrick's Day

**THE WORLD ALMANAC**

## THIS WEEK IN CELEBRITY BIRTHDAYS:

**18** ............ Adam Levine (1979– )

**19** ............ Bruce Willis (1955– )

**20** ............ Fred Rogers (1928–2003)

**21** ............ Rosie O'Donnell (1962– )

**22** ............ Reese Witherspoon (1976– )

**23** ............ Kyrie Irving (1992– )

**24** ............ Jim Parsons (1973– )

**18/19**

SAT/SUN
**MARCH**
**2023**

/Mothering Sunday (Ireland, UK)

**TODAY IN HISTORY**

In 1922, the first U.S. Navy aircraft carrier, USS *Langley*, was commissioned.

**20**

**MONDAY**
**MARCH**
**2023**

Vernal Equinox

## TODAY IN SPORTS HISTORY

In 1989, *Sports Illustrated* reported evidence linking the all-time MLB hits leader, player-manager Pete Rose, with illegal gambling on baseball games.

# THE WORLD ALMANAC

## World's Largest Muslim Populations
### (2022)

| Rank | Country | Muslim population | % of country's population |
|------|---------|-------------------|---------------------------|
| 1. | Pakistan | 221.6 | 96.6 |
| 2. | Indonesia | 221.6 | 79.4 |
| 3. | India | 207.0 | 14.7 |
| 4. | Bangladesh | 149.1 | 88.8 |
| 5. | Nigeria | 100.4 | 46.3 |

**22**

**WEDNESDAY**
**MARCH**
**2023**

Ramadan

**THE WORLD ALMANAC**

### TODAY IN HISTORY

In 2010, President Barack Obama signed into law the controversial Patient Protection and Affordable Care Act, which would enact sweeping health care reform measures under the informal name Obamacare.

**23**

**THURSDAY**
**MARCH**
**2023**

## BY THE NUMBERS

As recently as 1970, the U.S. had fewer than 200,000 people imprisoned nationwide, or less than 1 in 1,000 residents. That number rose steadily from the 1970s on, reaching an all-time high of more than 1.62 million prisoners in 2009 before beginning to decline.

**24**

**FRIDAY**
**MARCH**
**2023**

# THE WORLD ALMANAC

## THIS WEEK IN CELEBRITY BIRTHDAYS:

**25** ............ Aretha Franklin (1942–2018)

**26** ............ Diana Ross (1944– )

**27** ............ Mariah Carey (1969– )

**28** ............ Lady Gaga (1986– )

**29** ............ Cy Young (1867–1955)

**30** ............ Vincent Van Gogh (1853–1890)

**31** ............ Ewan McGregor (1971– )

# 25/26

SAT/SUN
**MARCH**
**2023**

## TODAY IN HISTORY

In 1964, the most powerful recorded earthquake in U.S. history (magnitude 9.2) struck Alaska, killing more than 100 people.

**27**

**MONDAY**
**MARCH**
**2023**

### TODAY IN SPORTS HISTORY

In 1984, the NFL's Baltimore Colts franchise moved to Indianapolis.

# THE WORLD ALMANAC

**BY THE NUMBERS**

The entire area of Arlington County, Virginia, is only twenty-six square miles, making it the smallest U.S. county.

**29**

**TODAY IN HISTORY**

In 1964, the TV game show *Jeopardy!* premiered on NBC, with original host Art Fleming.

# 30

**THURSDAY**
**MARCH**
**2023**

## THE WORLD ALMANAC

### Most Popular U.S. Dog Breeds
(2020)

1. Labrador Retrievers
2. French Bulldogs
3. German Shepherds
4. Golden Retrievers
5. Bulldogs

**31** | FRIDAY
**MARCH**
2023

## THIS WEEK IN CELEBRITY BIRTHDAYS:

**1** ............. David Oyelowo (1976– )

**2** ............. Christopher Meloni (1961– )

**3** ............. Eddie Murphy (1961– )

**4** ............. Robert Downey Jr. (1965– )

**5** ............. Lily James (1989– )

**6** ............. Paul Rudd (1969– )

**7** ............. Jackie Chan (1954– )

# 1/2

**SAT/SUN**
**APRIL**
**2023**

/Palm Sunday

# THE WORLD ALMANAC

### TODAY IN HISTORY

In 1973, a Motorola engineer made the first call with a handheld mobile cellular phone. He called a competitor at Bell Labs.

**3**

**MONDAY**
**APRIL**
**2023**

## THE WORLD ALMANAC

**TODAY IN SPORTS HISTORY**

In 1974, Hank Aaron hit his 714$^{th}$ home run, tying Babe Ruth's career record.

**4**

**TUESDAY**
**APRIL**
**2023**

# THE WORLD ALMANAC

## BY THE NUMBERS

Mount Waialeale in Kauai, Hawai'i, is considered to be the rainiest spot in the U.S. Over a thirty-year period, it averaged 460 inches of rain per year.

**5**

**WEDNESDAY**
**APRIL**
**2023**

Passover (begins at sundown)

**TODAY IN HISTORY**

In 1896, the first modern Olympic Games opened in Athens, Greece.

**6** | **THURSDAY**
**APRIL**
**2023**

The standard Protestant Old Testament consists of the same thirty-nine books as in the Bible of Judaism, but the latter is organized differently. The Old Testament used by Roman Catholics has seven additional deuterocanonical books (Tobit, Judith, Wisdom, Sirach [Ecclesiasticus], Baruch, I Maccabees, and II Maccabees), plus some additional parts of books.

**7**

**FRIDAY**
**APRIL**
**2023**

Good Friday (Western)

## THE WORLD ALMANAC

## THIS WEEK IN CELEBRITY BIRTHDAYS:

**8** .............. Patricia Arquette (1968– )

**9** .............. Kristen Stewart (1990– )

**10** ............ Mandy Moore (1984– )

**11** ............ Joel Grey (1932– )

**12** ............ David Letterman (1947– )

**13** ............ Thomas Jefferson (1743–1826)

**14** ............ Rob McElhenney (1977– )

# 8/9

**SAT/SUN**
**APRIL**
**2023**

/Easter (Western)

THE WORLD ALMANAC

**TODAY IN HISTORY**

In 1972, famed film comedian and director Charlie Chaplin received an honorary Oscar.

**10**

**MONDAY**
**APRIL**
**2023**

Easter Monday
(Australia, Canada, Ireland, NZ, UK—except Scotland)

# THE WORLD ALMANAC

## TODAY IN SPORTS HISTORY

In 1936, the Detroit Red Wings defeated the Toronto Maple Leafs to win their first Stanley Cup.

**11**

**TUESDAY**
**APRIL**
**2023**

**BY THE NUMBERS**

With a minimum of thirty-eight days off (including public holidays and statutory paid days off), Austria and Malta lead the world with the most days off given to workers.

**12** | **WEDNESDAY**
**APRIL**
**2023**

**THE WORLD ALMANAC**

**TODAY IN HISTORY**

In 1943, the Jefferson Memorial was dedicated in Washington, D.C., on the 200$^{th}$ anniversary of Thomas Jefferson's birth.

**13**

**THURSDAY**
**APRIL**
**2023**

Passover ends

In physics, dark energy is a mysterious, undefined energy leading to a repulsive force pervading all of space-time. Proposed by cosmologists as counteracting gravity and accelerating the expansion of the universe, it is theorized to make up 68.3 percent of the universe's composition.

**14**

**FRIDAY
APRIL
2023**

Holy Friday (Orthodox)

**THE WORLD ALMANAC**

## THIS WEEK IN CELEBRITY BIRTHDAYS:

**15** ............ Bessie Smith (1894–1937)

**16** ............ Chance the Rapper (1993– )

**17** ............ Jennifer Garner (1972– )

**18** ............ Conan O'Brien (1963– )

**19** ............ Kate Hudson (1979– )

**20** ............ George Takei (1937– )

**21** ............ James McAvoy (1979– )

**15/16** | SAT/SUN
**APRIL**
**2023**

/Easter (Orthodox)

# THE WORLD ALMANAC

**TODAY IN HISTORY**

In 1524, Italian navigator Giovanni da Verrazzano, sailing for France, led the first European expedition into the Bay of New York.

**17**

**MONDAY**
**APRIL**
**2023**

Yom HaShoah (begins at sundown)

**TODAY IN SPORTS HISTORY**

In 1923, Yankee Stadium, the "House That Ruth Built," opened to 74,200 baseball fans in the Bronx, New York.

**18**

**TUESDAY**
**APRIL**
**2023**

# THE WORLD ALMANAC

**BY THE NUMBERS**

Absolute zero is the theoretical temperature at which all motion within a molecule stops, corresponding to –273.15°C (–459.67°F).

**19**

**WEDNESDAY**
**APRIL**
**2023**

**TODAY IN HISTORY**

In 1902, Marie and Pierre Curie isolated the radioactive element radium for the first time.

**20**

**THURSDAY**
**APRIL**
**2023**

# THE WORLD ALMANAC

The date of Earth Day (April 22) was deliberately chosen in part as an appeal to college students' participation; it falls after spring break and before final exams at most universities.

**21** | **FRIDAY**
**APRIL**
**2023**

Eid al-Fitr

# THE WORLD ALMANAC

## THIS WEEK IN CELEBRITY BIRTHDAYS:

**22** ............ Jack Nicholson (1937– )

**23** ............ George Lopez (1961– )

**24** ............ Barbra Streisand (1942– )

**25** ............ Renée Zellweger (1969– )

**26** ............ Channing Tatum (1980– )

**27** ............ Lizzo (1988– )

**28** ............ Harper Lee (1926–2016)

# 22/23

**SAT/SUN**
**APRIL**
**2023**

Earth Day/
/St. George's Day (UK)

## THE WORLD ALMANAC

**TODAY IN HISTORY**

In 1913, New York City's Woolworth Building opened as the world's tallest building. The 58-story structure was 792 feet (241 meters) tall.

**24**

# THE WORLD ALMANAC

## TODAY IN SPORTS HISTORY

In 1950, Chuck Cooper became the first Black player drafted into the NBA when he was signed by the Boston Celtics.

## 25

**TUESDAY**
**APRIL**
**2023**

Anzac Day (NZ, Australia)

**THE WORLD ALMANAC**

## BY THE NUMBERS

The lowest point of elevation in most states is a body of water (near or below sea level). The lowest point of elevation in California is Death Valley at 282 feet below sea level.

**26** | **WEDNESDAY**
**APRIL**
**2023**

**TODAY IN HISTORY**

In 1865, the severely overcrowded steamboat *Sultana* exploded on the Mississippi River, killing some 1,800 passengers.

**27**

# THE WORLD ALMANAC

## Tallest Mountains in South America

| Peak, country | Height (feet) |
| --- | --- |
| Aconcagua, Argentina | 22,831 |
| Ojos del Salado, Argentina–Chile | 22,569 |
| Bonete, Argentina | 22,546 |
| Tupungato, Argentina–Chile | 22,310 |
| Pissis, Argentina | 22,241 |

# THE WORLD ALMANAC

## THIS WEEK IN CELEBRITY BIRTHDAYS:

**4/29** ........ Jerry Seinfeld (1954– )

**4/30** ........ Gal Gadot (1985– )

**5/1** .......... Tim McGraw (1967– )

**5/2** .......... Dwayne "The Rock" Johnson (1972– )

**5/3** .......... Brooks Koepka (1990– )

**5/4** .......... Audrey Hepburn (1929–1993)

**5/5** .......... Adele (1988– )

# 29/30

**SAT/SUN**
**APRIL**
**2023**

# THE WORLD ALMANAC

## TODAY IN HISTORY

In 1893, the World's Columbian Exposition officially opened to the public in Chicago. The World's Fair would draw more than 25 million visitors during its six-month run.

**1**

**MONDAY**
**MAY**
**2023**

May Day (Australia—NT)
Labour Day (Australia—QLD)
Early May Bank Holiday (Ireland, UK)

THE **WORLD ALMANAC**

### TODAY IN SPORTS HISTORY

In 1939, New York Yankee first baseman Lou Gehrig benched himself, bringing his record-setting streak of consecutive games played to a close at 2,130. Already suffering symptoms from ALS, now also commonly known as Lou Gehrig's disease, he never played another game.

**2**

**TUESDAY**
**MAY**
**2023**

**THE WORLD ALMANAC**

### BY THE NUMBERS

The speed of sound varies depending on temperature and the medium through which the sound travels. Sound moves faster in water than in air, for example. At sea level and a temperature of 59°F (15°C), the speed of sound is approximately 761 miles per hour, or 1,100 feet per second.

**3**

**WEDNESDAY**
**MAY**
**2023**

**TODAY IN HISTORY**

In 1959, the first Grammy Awards ceremony was held in
Los Angeles.

The American tarantula, a large, hairy spider, and probably all other tarantulas are harmless to humans, though their bite may cause some pain and swelling.

**5** | **FRIDAY**
**MAY**
**2023**

## THIS WEEK IN CELEBRITY BIRTHDAYS:

**6** ............. George Clooney (1961– )

**7** ............. J Balvin (1985– )

**8** ............. Thomas Pynchon (1937– )

**9** ............. Billy Joel (1949– )

**10** ........... Hélio Castroneves (1975– )

**11** ........... Cam Newton (1989– )

**12** ........... Rami Malek (1981– )

**6/7**

**SAT/SUN**
**MAY**
**2023**

## THE WORLD ALMANAC

### TODAY IN HISTORY

In 1877, the first dog show presented by the Westminster Kennel Club opened in New York City, drawing 1,201 dogs across all breeds.

**8**

**TODAY IN SPORTS HISTORY**

In 1984, the Chicago White Sox finally defeated the Milwaukee Brewers in a 25-inning game that began the previous evening (it was suspended after 17 innings). It was the longest timed game in MLB history, at 8 hours and 6 minutes.

**9**

# THE WORLD ALMANAC

## BY THE NUMBERS

In 1995, 67.0 percent of U.S. airline seats were occupied by passengers during scheduled service. By 2019, that number had risen to 84.6 percent.

**10** | **WEDNESDAY**
**MAY**
**2023**

# THE WORLD ALMANAC

## TODAY IN HISTORY

In 1910, President William Howard Taft signed legislation establishing Glacier National Park.

**11**

**THURSDAY**
**MAY**
**2023**

# THE WORLD ALMANAC

Plasma is a high-energy state of matter—different from solid, liquid, or gas—in which atomic nuclei and the electrons orbiting them separate from one another.

**12**

# THE WORLD ALMANAC

## THIS WEEK IN CELEBRITY BIRTHDAYS:

**13** ........... Bea Arthur (1922–2009)

**14** ........... Rob Gronkowski (1989– )

**15** ........... Emmitt Smith (1969– )

**16** ........... Janet Jackson (1966– )

**17** ........... Dennis Hopper (1936–2010)

**18** ........... Tina Fey (1970– )

**19** ........... Sam Smith (1992– )

## 13/14

**SAT/SUN**
**MAY**
**2023**

/Mother's Day
(USA, Australia, Canada, NZ)

# THE WORLD ALMANAC

**TODAY IN HISTORY**

In 1918, the U.S. Post Office launched its first regular scheduled airmail service, between New York and Washington, D.C.

**15**

**MONDAY**
**MAY**
**2023**

### TODAY IN SPORTS HISTORY

In 1980, rookie Earvin "Magic" Johnson, filling in for an injured Kareem Abdul-Jabbar, scored 42 points in the Los Angeles Lakers' NBA Championship win.

**16**

**TUESDAY**
**MAY**
**2023**

## BY THE NUMBERS

Baku, Azerbaijan, located at 92 feet below sea level, is the lowest national capital city in the world. With a population of over 2.3 million, Baku is also the largest city in the world located below sea level.

**THE WORLD ALMANAC**

### TODAY IN HISTORY

In 1917, President Woodrow Wilson signed the Selective Service Act into law, requiring that all men aged 21–30 register for military service.

**18**

**THURSDAY**
**MAY**
**2023**

The first member of Congress to give birth while serving in office was Representative Yvonne Brathwaite Burke (D–California, 1973–79), who had a daughter on November 23, 1973. She also became the first member of Congress to be granted maternity leave.

**19** | **FRIDAY**
**MAY**
**2023**

**THIS WEEK IN CELEBRITY BIRTHDAYS:**

**20** ........... Cher (1946– )

**21** ........... Mr. T (1952– )

**22** ........... Novak Djokovic (1987– )

**23** ........... Drew Carey (1958– )

**24** ........... Patti LaBelle (1944– )

**25** ........... Octavia Spencer (1970– )

**26** ........... John Wayne (1907–1979)

# 20/21

**SAT/SUN**
**MAY**
**2023**

Armed Forces Day (USA)/

## THE WORLD ALMANAC

**TODAY IN HISTORY**

In 1992, 50 million viewers watched as Johnny Carson signed off as *The Tonight Show* host for the last time.

**22**

Victoria Day (Canada)

**TODAY IN SPORTS HISTORY**

In 1895, the Louisville Colonels forfeited a home game to the Brooklyn Bridegrooms because they ran out of baseballs in the third inning.

**23** TUESDAY
**MAY**
**2023**

## BY THE NUMBERS

Though a 1911 act of Congress fixed the number of representatives in the U.S. Congress at 435, Alaska and Hawai'i each gained one House seat when they became states, temporarily raising the total to 437 representatives until after the 1960 census was conducted.

## 24 | WEDNESDAY MAY 2023

**TODAY IN HISTORY**

In 1977, the first *Star Wars* movie was released in American theaters.

**25** | **THURSDAY**
**MAY**
**2023**

# THE WORLD ALMANAC

Memorial Day did not become an official federal holiday in the U.S. until 1971, but its origins date back to the Civil War.

# THE WORLD ALMANAC

## THIS WEEK IN CELEBRITY BIRTHDAYS:

**5/27** ........ Jamie Oliver (1975– )

**5/28** ........ Kylie Minogue (1968– )

**5/29** ........ John F. Kennedy (1917–1963)

**5/30** ........ Idina Menzel (1971– )

**5/31** ........ Colin Farrell (1976– )

**6/1** .......... Tom Holland (1996– )

**6/2** .......... Andy Cohen (1968– )

## 27/28

SAT/SUN
**MAY**
**2023**

**THE WORLD ALMANAC**

## TODAY IN HISTORY

In 1913, Igor Stravinsky's *The Rite of Spring*, choreographed by Vaslav Nijinsky for Ballets Russes, sparked a near-riot at its Paris premiere.

**29**

**MONDAY**
**MAY**
**2023**

Memorial Day (USA)
Bank Holiday (UK)

# THE WORLD ALMANAC

## TODAY IN SPORTS HISTORY

In 1904, the Chicago Cubs' Frank Chance was hit by four different wild pitches during a doubleheader against Cincinnati.

**30** | **TUESDAY**
**MAY**
**2023**

**THE WORLD ALMANAC**

### BY THE NUMBERS

The first U.S. census, conducted in 1790, counted the numbers of free white males ages 16 and over (as a measure of available workers and military personnel), free white males under 16, free white females, all other free persons, and enslaved persons.

**31** | **WEDNESDAY**
**MAY**
**2023**

**TODAY IN HISTORY**

In 1980, Cable News Network (CNN) launched as the first-ever 24-hour news channel.

**1**

**THURSDAY**
**JUNE**
**2023**

## World's Tallest Buildings
(2021)

| Building (year completed) | Height (feet) | Stories |
|---|---|---|
| Burj Khalifa, Dubai, United Arab Emirates (2010) | 2,717 | 163 |
| *Merdeka PNB 118, Kuala Lumpur, Malaysia (2022) | 2,113 | 118 |
| Shanghai Tower, Shanghai, China (2015) | 2,074 | 128 |
| Makkah Royal Clock Tower Hotel, Mecca, Saudi Arabia (2013) | 1,972 | 120 |
| Ping An Finance Center, Shenzhen, China (2016) | 1,965 | 115 |

* = Under construction as of 2021.

**2**

**FRIDAY**
**JUNE**
**2023**

**THE WORLD ALMANAC**

## THIS WEEK IN CELEBRITY BIRTHDAYS:

**3** .............. Rafael Nadal (1986– )

**4** .............. Angelina Jolie (1975– )

**5** .............. Suze Orman (1951– )

**6** .............. Björn Borg (1956– )

**7** .............. Bill Hader (1978– )

**8** .............. Ye, AKA Kanye West (1977– )

**9** .............. Michael J. Fox (1961– )

# 3/4

**SAT/SUN**
**JUNE**
**2023**

# THE WORLD ALMANAC

**TODAY IN HISTORY**

In 1968, Senator Robert F. Kennedy (D–New York) was fatally shot in Los Angeles while campaigning for the Democratic presidential nomination.

**5**

**MONDAY**
**JUNE**
**2023**

Queen's Birthday (NZ)
Bank Holiday (Ireland)

## THE WORLD ALMANAC

**TODAY IN SPORTS HISTORY**

In 2015, American Pharoah became the first horse in 37 years (and 12th of all time) to claim thoroughbred racing's Triple Crown after winning the 147th Belmont Stakes in Elmont, NY.

**6** | **TUESDAY**
**JUNE**
**2023**

**BY THE NUMBERS**

The number of justices on the U.S. Supreme Court changed six times before settling at a total of nine in 1869. Since 1803, the Court has declared more than 180 acts of Congress and over 1,000 state, territorial, and municipal laws and statutes to be unconstitutional.

**7** | **WEDNESDAY**
**JUNE**
**2023**

# THE WORLD ALMANAC

### TODAY IN HISTORY

In 1789, James Madison, then a member of the U.S. House of Representatives, proposed the Bill of Rights to Congress as amendments to the Constitution.

**8**

# THE WORLD ALMANAC

In physics, string theory seeks to unify quantum mechanics and general relativity, positing that the basic constituents of matter can best be understood not as pointlike particles but as tiny oscillating "strings."

**9**

**FRIDAY**
**JUNE**
**2023**

**THIS WEEK IN CELEBRITY BIRTHDAYS:**

**10** ............ Judy Garland (1922–1969)

**11** ............ Peter Dinklage (1969– )

**12** ............ George H. W. Bush (1924–2018)

**13** ............ Chris Evans (1981– )

**14** ............ Lucy Hale (1989– )

**15** ............ Courteney Cox (1964– )

**16** ............ Phil Mickelson (1970– )

**10/11** | SAT/SUN
**JUNE**
**2023**

**TODAY IN HISTORY**

In 1987, President Ronald Reagan instructed Soviet leader Mikhail Gorbachev to "tear down this wall" in a speech delivered in divided Berlin.

**12**

**MONDAY**
**JUNE**
**2023**

Queen's Birthday (Australia—except QLD, WA)

**TODAY IN SPORTS HISTORY**

In 1948, Babe Ruth's jersey number was ceremonially retired at Yankee Stadium in New York.

**13**

Until an Executive Order of June 24, 1912, by President William Howard Taft, neither the order of the stars nor the proportions of the American flag were standardized. Flags dating before this period thus sometimes show unusual arrangements of stars and odd proportions.

**14**

**WEDNESDAY**
**JUNE**
**2023**

Flag Day (USA)

## THE WORLD ALMANAC

**TODAY IN HISTORY**

In 1846, Britain and the U.S. settled the boundary dispute between the U.S. and Canada in the Pacific Northwest.

**15**

**THURSDAY**
**JUNE**
**2023**

The internet is not owned or funded by any one institution, organization, or government. It has no CEO and is not a commercial service. Its development is guided by the Internet Society (ISOC), a nonprofit formed in 1992.

**16**

**FRIDAY**
**JUNE**
**2023**

## THIS WEEK IN CELEBRITY BIRTHDAYS:

**17** ............ Kendrick Lamar (1987– )

**18** ............ Paul McCartney (1942– )

**19** ............ Jacob deGrom (1988– )

**20** ............ Nicole Kidman (1967– )

**21** ............ Prince William (1982– )

**22** ............ Dan Brown (1964– )

**23** ............ Frances McDormand (1957– )

# 17/18

**SAT/SUN**
**JUNE**
**2023**

/Father's Day (USA, Canada, Ireland, UK)

## THE WORLD ALMANAC

**TODAY IN HISTORY**

In 1978, the comic strip *Garfield* debuted in forty-one U.S. newspapers.

**19**

**MONDAY**
**JUNE**
**2023**

Juneteenth (USA)

**THE WORLD ALMANAC**

## TODAY IN SPORTS HISTORY

In 1967, boxer Muhammad Ali was convicted of violating federal law by refusing to be inducted into the Army. (Ali's conviction was overturned by the U.S. Supreme Court in 1971.)

**20**

**TUESDAY**
**JUNE**
**2023**

## BY THE NUMBERS

Just twenty-four pitchers in Major League Baseball history have achieved a milestone 300 career wins.

**21** | **WEDNESDAY**
**JUNE**
**2023**

Summer Solstice
National Indigenous Peoples Day (Canada)

# THE WORLD ALMANAC

**TODAY IN HISTORY**

In 1944, President Franklin D. Roosevelt signed the G.I. Bill of Rights, which provided certain benefits to veterans returning from World War II service.

**22**

# THE WORLD ALMANAC

Antimatter is matter that consists of antiparticles, such as antiprotons, that have an opposite charge from normal particles. When matter meets antimatter, both are destroyed, and their combined mass is converted to energy. Antimatter is created in certain radioactive decay processes but appears to be present in only small amounts in the universe.

**23**

**FRIDAY
JUNE
2023**

# THE WORLD ALMANAC

## THIS WEEK IN CELEBRITY BIRTHDAYS:

**24** ........... Solange Knowles (1986– )

**25** ........... Ricky Gervais (1961– )

**26** ........... Ariana Grande (1993– )

**27** ........... Vera Wang (1949– )

**28** ........... Elon Musk (1971– )

**29** ........... Kawhi Leonard (1991– )

**30** ........... Michael Phelps (1985– )

# 24/25

**SAT/SUN**
**JUNE**
**2023**

**TODAY IN HISTORY**

In 2000, scientists announced the completion of a basic structural map of the human genome.

**26** | **MONDAY**
**JUNE**
**2023**

# THE WORLD ALMANAC

**TODAY IN SPORTS HISTORY**

In 1988, Mike Tyson knocked out Michael Spinks just ninety-one seconds into the first round.

**27** | **TUESDAY**
**JUNE**
**2023**

**BY THE NUMBERS**

The longest river system in the U.S. is the Mississippi–Missouri–Red Rock, which covers 3,710 miles.

**28**

Eid al-Adha

**TODAY IN HISTORY**

In 2007, the first-generation Apple iPhone was released to the public.

## Tallest Mountains in Africa

| Peak, country | Height (feet) |
| --- | --- |
| Kilimanjaro, Tanzania | 19,341 |
| Kenya, Kenya | 17,057 |
| Margherita Peak, Uganda–Congo | 16,765 |
| Meru, Tanzania | 14,977 |
| Ras Dashen, Ethiopia | 14,872 |

**30** FRIDAY
JUNE
2023

## THIS WEEK IN CELEBRITY BIRTHDAYS:

**1** .............. Olivia de Havilland (1916–2020)

**2** .............. Margot Robbie (1990– )

**3** .............. Tom Cruise (1962– )

**4** .............. Bill Withers (1938–2020)

**5** .............. Edie Falco (1963– )

**6** .............. Kevin Hart (1979– )

**7** .............. Ringo Starr (1940– )

**1/2**

**SAT/SUN**
**JULY**
**2023**

Canada Day/

**TODAY IN HISTORY**

In 1775, George Washington assumed command of the Continental Army.

**3** | **MONDAY**
**JULY**
**2023**

# THE WORLD ALMANAC

## TODAY IN SPORTS HISTORY

In 1939, close to 62,000 baseball fans honored Lou Gehrig, who was suffering from amyotrophic lateral sclerosis (ALS), at Yankee Stadium. Gehrig delivered the famous line, "Today, I consider myself the luckiest man on the face of the earth."

**4**

**TUESDAY**
**JULY**
**2023**

Independence Day (USA)

## BY THE NUMBERS

Eruptions have been confirmed in some 560 volcanoes. More than half to three-quarters of historically active volcanoes can be found on the so-called Ring of Fire, which runs along the western coast of the Americas from the southern tip of Chile to Alaska, down the eastern coast of Asia from Kamchatka to Indonesia, and continues from New Guinea to New Zealand.

**5**

**WEDNESDAY**
**JULY**
**2023**

# THE WORLD ALMANAC

**TODAY IN HISTORY**

In 1885, Louis Pasteur successfully tested his vaccine against rabies in a human subject.

**6**

# THE WORLD ALMANAC

Contrary to popular myth, out of nearly 1,000 bat species, only three feed on blood (mostly cattle blood).

**7** | **FRIDAY**
**JULY**
**2023**

## THIS WEEK IN CELEBRITY BIRTHDAYS:

**8** .............. Kevin Bacon (1958– )

**9** .............. Tom Hanks (1956– )

**10** ............ Sofía Vergara (1972– )

**11** ............ E. B. White (1899–1985)

**12** ............ Malala Yousafzai (1997– )

**13** ............ Harrison Ford (1942– )

**14** ............ Jane Lynch (1960– )

**8/9** | **SAT/SUN**
**JULY**
**2023**

## THE WORLD ALMANAC

### TODAY IN HISTORY

In 1940, Nazi forces began an air attack on the UK that would last 114 days and become known as the Battle of Britain.

**10**

**MONDAY**
**JULY**
**2023**

**TODAY IN SPORTS HISTORY**

In 1985, during a 4–3 victory over the New York Mets, Houston Astros pitcher Nolan Ryan became the first major league pitcher to record 4,000 career strikeouts.

**11** | **TUESDAY**
**JULY**
**2023**

**THE WORLD ALMANAC**

### BY THE NUMBERS

The record low (recorded) temperature in the U.S. was −80°F at Prospect Creek, Alaska, on January 23, 1971.

**12**

**WEDNESDAY**
**JULY**
**2023**

# THE WORLD ALMANAC

The "Hollywoodland" sign was completed in the hills above Los Angeles, California, during the summer of 1923. (The last four letters were dropped from the sign in 1949.)

**13**

Because Venus is almost the same size as Earth, it is believed that the two planets were formed at the same time by the same general process and from the same mixture of chemical elements. Venus can easily be seen from Earth with the naked eye; it is the third-brightest object in Earth's sky, exceeded only by the sun and the moon.

**14**

**FRIDAY**
**JULY**
**2023**

# THE WORLD ALMANAC

## THIS WEEK IN CELEBRITY BIRTHDAYS:

**15** ............ Forest Whitaker (1961– )

**16** ............ Will Ferrell (1967– )

**17** ............ Angela Merkel (1954– )

**18** ............ Nelson Mandela (1918–2013)

**19** ............ Benedict Cumberbatch (1976– )

**20** ............ Sandra Oh (1971– )

**21** ............ Robin Williams (1951–2014)

# 15/16

**SAT/SUN**
**JULY**
**2023**

### TODAY IN HISTORY

In 1945, U.S. President Harry S. Truman, USSR Premier Joseph Stalin, and UK Prime Minister Winston Churchill began meetings now known as the Potsdam Conference to discuss postwar Europe and the ongoing war in the Pacific.

**17**

**MONDAY**
**JULY**
**2023**

## THE WORLD ALMANAC

**TODAY IN SPORTS HISTORY**

In 1976, Nadia Comaneci of Romania scored a perfect 10 in the uneven parallel bars, becoming the first gymnast to ever achieve a perfect score in Olympic competition.

**18**

# THE WORLD ALMANAC

Construction on the International Space Station (ISS) began in 1998 and was completed in 2011. It has been inhabited continuously since 2000 and visited by more than 244 international crew members from nineteen countries.

# THE WORLD ALMANAC

**TODAY IN HISTORY**

In 1969, Neil Armstrong, commander of *Apollo 11*, became the first person to set foot on the moon, followed by Buzz Aldrin.

## 20

**THURSDAY**
**JULY**
**2023**

# THE WORLD ALMANAC

## Tallest Mountains in North America

| Peak, state/province, country | Height (feet) |
| --- | --- |
| Denali (fmr. McKinley), Alaska, U.S. | 20,310 |
| Logan, Yukon, Canada | 19,551 |
| Pico de Orizaba, Mexico | 18,619 |
| St. Elias, Alaska–Yukon, U.S.–Canada | 18,009 |
| Popocatépetl, Mexico | 17,802 |

**THE WORLD ALMANAC**

## THIS WEEK IN CELEBRITY BIRTHDAYS:

**22** ........... Selena Gomez (1992– )

**23** ........... Daniel Radcliffe (1989– )

**24** ........... Jennifer Lopez (1969– )

**25** ........... Matt LeBlanc (1967– )

**26** ........... Mick Jagger (1943– )

**27** ........... Alex Rodriguez (1975– )

**28** ........... Jacqueline Kennedy Onassis (1929–1994)

# 22/23

**SAT/SUN**
**JULY**
**2023**

# THE WORLD ALMANAC

## TODAY IN HISTORY

In 1959, Vice President Richard Nixon and Soviet Premier Nikita Khrushchev engaged in what became known as the "kitchen debate."

**24**

# THE WORLD ALMANAC

## TODAY IN SPORTS HISTORY

In 1976, American Edwin Moses ran in his first international track-and-field event at the Montréal Olympics—the 400-meter hurdles—and won a gold medal with a world record–setting time.

## TODAY IN SPORTS HISTORY

# THE WORLD ALMANAC

## BY THE NUMBERS

The continent of Antarctica, with an area of about 5.48 million square miles (of which 110,039 square miles are ice-free), is generally considered a desert. Average annual precipitation for the continent as a whole is two to six inches, with most precipitation falling along the coast; there is little evaporation.

**26**

**WEDNESDAY**
**JULY**
**2023**

# THE WORLD ALMANAC

## TODAY IN HISTORY

In 1974, the House of Representatives Committee on the Judiciary voted to recommend the first of three articles of impeachment against President Richard Nixon.

**27**

# THE WORLD ALMANAC

The International Hydrographic Organization delimited a fifth world ocean in 2000. The Southern (Antarctic) Ocean extends from the coast of Antarctica north to 60°S latitude, encompassing portions of the Atlantic, Indian, and Pacific Oceans.

**28**

FRIDAY
JULY
2023

# THE WORLD ALMANAC

## THIS WEEK IN CELEBRITY BIRTHDAYS:

**7/29** ........ Tim Gunn (1953– )

**7/30** ........ Lisa Kudrow (1963– )

**7/31** ........ Mark Cuban (1958– )

**8/1** .......... Jason Momoa (1979– )

**8/2** .......... James Baldwin (1924–1987)

**8/3** .......... Tom Brady (1977– )

**8/4** .......... Meghan, Duchess of Sussex (1981– )

# 29/30

**SAT/SUN**
**JULY**
**2023**

# THE WORLD ALMANAC

**TODAY IN HISTORY**

In 1991, U.S. President George H. W. Bush and Soviet President Mikhail Gorbachev signed the START Treaty, which was the first ever to mandate reductions in strategic nuclear arms by the two powers.

## 31 | MONDAY JULY 2023

# ┴WORLD ALMANAC

## TODAY IN SPORTS HISTORY

In 1936, the Olympic Games opened in Berlin before a crowd of 100,000 spectators presided over by Chancellor Adolf Hitler.

**1**

**TUESDAY**
**AUGUST**
**2023**

# THE WORLD ALMANAC

## BY THE NUMBERS

The U.S. Postal Service first introduced the "Forever" stamp in 2007, at an initial cost of forty-one cents.

**2** | **WEDNESDAY**
**AUGUST**
**2023**

# THE WORLD ALMANAC

**TODAY IN HISTORY**

In 1958, the nuclear-powered submarine USS *Nautilus* became the first vessel to cross the North Pole underwater.

# THE WORLD ALMANAC

Gas giant planets like Jupiter, Saturn, and Neptune do not have a surface like Earth or any of the other rocky planets. The gases become denser with depth, until they may turn into a slush or slurry.

**4**

**THIS WEEK IN CELEBRITY BIRTHDAYS:**

**5** .............. Neil Armstrong (1930–2012)

**6** .............. Lucille Ball (1911–1989)

**7** .............. Sidney Crosby (1987– )

**8** .............. Shawn Mendes (1998– )

**9** .............. Hoda Kotb (1964– )

**10** ............ Kylie Jenner (1997– )

**11** ............ Viola Davis (1965– )

**5/6**

SAT/SUN
**AUGUST**
2023

**THE WORLD ALMANAC**

### TODAY IN HISTORY

In 1964, Congress passed the Gulf of Tonkin Resolution, giving
President Lyndon Johnson wide discretionary power in responding
to reported Vietnamese attacks.

**7**

**MONDAY**
**AUGUST**
**2023**

Bank Holiday
(Ireland, UK–Scotland, Australia–NSW)
Picnic Day (Australia–NT)

### THE WORLD ALMANAC

**TODAY IN SPORTS HISTORY**

In 2008, the Summer Olympic Games opened in Beijing, China.

**8**

# THE WORLD ALMANAC

**BY THE NUMBERS**

As of 2021, there were 193 members of the United Nations. Palestine and Vatican City are non-member states of the UN with permanent observer status.

## THE WORLD ALMANAC

**TODAY IN HISTORY**

In 1988, President Ronald Reagan signed legislation that set up a framework for making reparations to Japanese Americans interned during World War II.

**10**

**THURSDAY**
**AUGUST**
**2023**

**THE WORLD ALMANAC**

A lake is generally defined as a body of water surrounded by land. By this definition, some bodies of water that are called seas—such as the Caspian Sea and the Aral Sea—are really lakes.

**11** | **FRIDAY**
**AUGUST**
**2023**

## THE WORLD ALMANAC

### THIS WEEK IN CELEBRITY BIRTHDAYS:

**12** ........... Cara Delevingne (1992– )

**13** ........... Alfred Hitchcock (1899–1980)

**14** ........... Magic Johnson (1959– )

**15** ........... Ben Affleck (1972– )

**16** ........... Madonna (1958– )

**17** ........... Phoebe Bridgers (1994– )

**18** ........... Andy Samberg (1978– )

# 12/13

SAT/SUN
**AUGUST**
**2023**

## THE WORLD ALMANAC

**TODAY IN HISTORY**

In 2003, some 50 million people in the northeastern U.S. and
Canada lost power in one of the largest blackouts in U.S. history.

**14**

**MONDAY**
**AUGUST**
**2023**

# THE WORLD ALMANAC

## TODAY IN SPORTS HISTORY

In 1948, famed multisport athlete "Babe" Didrikson Zaharias won the third U.S. Women's Open golf tournament. She would go on to win two more, in 1950 and 1954.

**15**

## THE WORLD ALMANAC

### BY THE NUMBERS

The smallest state in the U.S. (Rhode Island, 1,545 square miles) would fit into the largest state in the U.S. (Alaska, 665,384 square miles) 430 times.

**16** | **WEDNESDAY**
**AUGUST**
**2023**

## THE WORLD ALMANAC

### TODAY IN HISTORY

In 1959, Miles Davis's *Kind of Blue* album was released.

**17**

**THURSDAY**
**AUGUST**
**2023**

# THE WORLD ALMANAC

When a chunk of material—ice or rock—plunges into Earth's atmosphere and burns up in a fiery display, the event is a meteor. While the chunk of material is still in space, it is a meteoroid. If a portion of the material survives passage through the atmosphere and reaches the ground, the remnant on the ground is a meteorite.

**18**

FRIDAY
**AUGUST**
2023

# THE WORLD ALMANAC

## THIS WEEK IN CELEBRITY BIRTHDAYS:

**19** ........... Matthew Perry (1969– )

**20** ........... Demi Lovato (1992– )

**21** ........... Usain Bolt (1986– )

**22** ........... Dua Lipa (1995– )

**23** ........... Kobe Bryant (1978–2020)

**24** ........... Rupert Grint (1988– )

**25** ........... Rachael Ray (1968– )

# 19/20

## THE WORLD ALMANAC

**TODAY IN HISTORY**

In 1858, Abraham Lincoln and Stephen Douglas, opponents in a race to fill one of Illinois's U.S. Senate seats, held the first of seven storied debates.

**21**

### TODAY IN SPORTS HISTORY

In 2007, the Texas Rangers routed the Baltimore Orioles, 30–3, to set a modern MLB record for most runs scored in a game. The Rangers had twenty-nine hits, including six home runs (two of which were grand slams).

**22**

**TUESDAY**
**AUGUST**
**2023**

## TODAY IN SPORTS HISTORY

**BY THE NUMBERS**

Dark matter is hypothetical, invisible matter that some scientists believe makes up 26.8 percent of the universe (dark matter and ordinary matter together make up 31.7 percent of the universe). Its existence was proposed to account for otherwise inexplicable gravitational forces observed in space.

**TODAY IN HISTORY**

In 1932, Amelia Earhart became the first woman to fly solo nonstop across North America.

The five zones of Earth's surface are the Torrid, lying between the Tropics of Cancer and Capricorn; the North Temperate, between Cancer and the Arctic Circle; the South Temperate, between Capricorn and the Antarctic Circle; and the two Frigid Zones, between the Polar Circles and the Poles.

**25**

**FRIDAY**
**AUGUST**
**2023**

## THE WORLD ALMANAC

### THIS WEEK IN CELEBRITY BIRTHDAYS:

**8/26** ........ Chris Pine (1980– )

**8/27** ........ Aaron Paul (1979– )

**8/28** ........ Shania Twain (1965– )

**8/29** ........ John McCain (1936–2018)

**8/30** ........ Cameron Diaz (1972– )

**8/31** ........ Richard Gere (1949– )

**9/1** .......... Zendaya (1996– )

# 26/27

**SAT/SUN**
**AUGUST**
**2023**

**TODAY IN HISTORY**

In 1963, the March on Washington drew hundreds of thousands of civil rights activists to Washington, D.C.

**28**

**MONDAY**
**AUGUST**
**2023**

Bank Holiday (UK—except Scotland)

## THE WORLD ALMANAC

### TODAY IN SPORTS HISTORY

In 1977, St. Louis Cardinals outfielder Lou Brock stole two bases to match, then break, Ty Cobb's record for career stolen bases, which had stood at 892 bases for forty-nine years.

**29**

## THE WORLD ALMANAC

**BY THE NUMBERS**

The Canadian side of Niagara Falls (Horseshoe Falls) has a height of 167 feet, while the American Falls are about 120 feet high.

**30**

**WEDNESDAY**
**AUGUST**
**2023**

BY THE NUMBERS

**TODAY IN HISTORY**

In 2001, the last original episode of *Mr. Rogers' Neighborhood* aired.

## Highest U.S. Dams

| Rank | Dam | River | Height (feet) |
|------|-----|-------|---------------|
| 1. | Oroville | Feather | 770 |
| 2. | Hoover | Colorado | 730 |
| 3. | Dworshak | North Fork Clearwater | 717 |
| 4. | Glen Canyon | Colorado | 710 |
| 5. | New Bullards Bar | North Yuba | 645 |

**1**

**FRIDAY**
**SEPTEMBER**
**2023**

# THE WORLD ALMANAC

## THIS WEEK IN CELEBRITY BIRTHDAYS:

**2** .............. Mark Harmon (1951– )

**3** .............. Charlie Sheen (1965– )

**4** .............. Beyoncé (1981– )

**5** .............. Michael Keaton (1951– )

**6** .............. Idris Elba (1972– )

**7** .............. Leslie Jones (1967– )

**8** .............. Patsy Cline (1932–1963)

# 2/3

**SAT/SUN**
**SEPTEMBER**
**2023**

/Father's Day (Australia, NZ)

**THE WORLD ALMANAC**

---

### TODAY IN HISTORY

In 1998, graduate students Sergey Brin and Larry Page filed paperwork to incorporate Google, their two-year-old research project, as a company.

**4**

**MONDAY**
**SEPTEMBER**
**2023**

Labor Day (USA, Canada)

## THE WORLD ALMANAC

**TODAY IN SPORTS HISTORY**

In 1960, Muhammad Ali (then competing as Cassius Clay) won the light heavyweight boxing gold medal at the Summer Olympic Games in Rome, Italy.

**5** | **TUESDAY**
**SEPTEMBER**
**2023**

# THE WORLD ALMANAC

**BY THE NUMBERS**

Stanford University researchers published a paper in 2019 with the finding that a blue whale's heart beat a maximum of just 35–37 times a minute (on the water's surface to restore oxygen levels, in the wild). When the whale dove, its heart rate slowed to a low of only 2–4 beats per minute.

**6** | **WEDNESDAY**
**SEPTEMBER**
**2023**

**TODAY IN HISTORY**

In 1979, cable sports network ESPN was launched; the first show aired was *SportsCenter*.

**7**

Female bats give birth upside down and catch the pup in their wings.

**8**

# THE WORLD ALMANAC

## THIS WEEK IN CELEBRITY BIRTHDAYS:

**9** .............. Adam Sandler (1966– )

**10** ........... Misty Copeland (1982– )

**11** ........... Taraji P. Henson (1970– )

**12** ........... Jennifer Hudson (1981– )

**13** ........... Jean Smart (1951– )

**14** ........... Amy Winehouse (1983–2011)

**15** ........... Prince Harry (1984– )

# 9/10

**SAT/SUN**
**SEPTEMBER**
**2023**

### THE WORLD ALMANAC

### TODAY IN HISTORY

In 1973, General Augusto Pinochet seized control of Chile in a military coup.

**11**

## THE WORLD ALMANAC

**TODAY IN SPORTS HISTORY**

In 1979, Boston Red Sox slugger Carl Yastrzemski became the first American League player to reach career totals of 3,000 hits and 400 homers.

**12**

**TUESDAY**
**SEPTEMBER**
**2023**

# THE WORLD ALMANAC

**BY THE NUMBERS**

There are more than 1,400 species in the cactus (cactaceae) family of plants. The largest, *Pachycereus pringlei* or elephant cactus, can grow up to sixty feet tall.

**13** | **WEDNESDAY**
**SEPTEMBER**
**2023**

# THE WORLD ALMANAC

**TODAY IN HISTORY**

In 1901, President William McKinley died of wounds from an assassin's bullet, and Vice President Theodore Roosevelt was sworn in as his successor.

**14**

**THURSDAY**
**SEPTEMBER**
**2023**

## THE WORLD ALMANAC

Since the founding of the United Nations in 1946, only nine people have served as its secretary-general. Four were from Europe, two were from Asia, two were from Africa, and one was from South America.

**15**

## THE WORLD ALMANAC

**THIS WEEK IN CELEBRITY BIRTHDAYS:**

**16** ............ Amy Poehler (1971– )

**17** ............ Alexander Ovechkin (1985– )

**18** ............ Jada Pinkett Smith (1971– )

**19** ............ Jimmy Fallon (1974– )

**20** ............ George R. R. Martin (1948– )

**21** ............ Bill Murray (1950– )

**22** ............ Tatiana Maslany (1985– )

# 16/17

**SAT/SUN**
**SEPTEMBER**
**2023**

/Rosh Hashanah ends

**THE WORLD ALMANAC**

### TODAY IN HISTORY

In 1851, *The New York Times* published its first edition, as the "New-York Daily Times."

**18**

## THE WORLD ALMANAC

**TODAY IN SPORTS HISTORY**

In 1988, U.S. Olympic diver Greg Louganis hit his head on the board during a dive. He came back to win gold at the Summer Olympic Games in Seoul, South Korea, just one day later.

**19**

**TUESDAY**
**SEPTEMBER**
**2023**

## THE WORLD ALMANAC

### BY THE NUMBERS

The sun is the biggest object in the Earth's solar system, 332,900 times more massive than Earth; it contains 99.86 percent of the mass of the entire solar system. On the whole, the sun is made up of about 92.1 percent hydrogen and 7.8 percent helium, with trace amounts of other elements.

**20**

**WEDNESDAY
SEPTEMBER
2023**

**THE WORLD ALMANAC**

**TODAY IN HISTORY**

In 1937, J. R. R. Tolkien's *The Hobbit* was first published.

**21**

**THURSDAY**
**SEPTEMBER**
**2023**

U.N. International Day of Peace

## Countries With the Smallest Populations
### (2021)

| Rank | Country | Population |
|------|---------|-----------|
| 1. | Vatican City* | 1,000 |
| 2. | Nauru | 9,770 |
| 3. | Tuvalu | 11,448 |
| 4. | Palau | 21,613 |
| 5. | Monaco | 31,223 |

* = As of mid-2019.

**22**

FRIDAY
**SEPTEMBER**
2023

**THIS WEEK IN CELEBRITY BIRTHDAYS:**

**23** ............ Bruce Springsteen (1949– )

**24** ............ Ben Platt (1993– )

**25** ............ Will Smith (1968– )

**26** ............ Serena Williams (1981– )

**27** ............ Gwyneth Paltrow (1972– )

**28** ............ Naomi Watts (1968– )

**29** ............ Halsey (1994– )

# 23/24

**SAT/SUN**
**SEPTEMBER**
**2023**

Autumnal Equinox/
/Yom Kippur (begins at sundown)

### TODAY IN HISTORY

In 1981, Sandra Day O'Connor was sworn in as the first woman to serve as a U.S. Supreme Court justice.

**25**

**MONDAY**
**SEPTEMBER**
**2023**

Queen's Birthday (Australia—WA)

**TODAY IN SPORTS HISTORY**

In 1983, the Royal Perth Yacht Club's *Australia II* won the America's Cup yacht race. It was the first win by a non-American yacht in the Cup's 132-year history.

**26**

**BY THE NUMBERS**

Pluto has five known natural satellites. Charon, the biggest, has a diameter of 750 miles—about half of Pluto's diameter of 1,474 miles. No other planet or dwarf planet has a moon so close to its size.

**27**

**TODAY IN HISTORY**

In 1928, Scottish physician and microbiologist Alexander Fleming observed some of the antibacterial characteristics of penicillin, a discovery that led to the first effective antibiotics.

**28**

In common usage, gravity refers to the gravitational force between planets and objects on or near them. But in scientific parlance, gravitation is one of four basic forces controlling the interactions of matter. (The others are the strong and weak forces, which act on the subatomic level, and the electromagnetic force.)

**29**

**FRIDAY**
**SEPTEMBER**
**2023**

## THIS WEEK IN CELEBRITY BIRTHDAYS:

**9/30**........ Monica Bellucci (1964– )

**10/1** ........ Brie Larson (1989– )

**10/2** ........ Kelly Ripa (1970– )

**10/3** ........ Gwen Stefani (1969– )

**10/4** ........ Dakota Johnson (1989– )

**10/5** ........ Kate Winslet (1975– )

**10/6** ........ Bill Buford (1954– )

**30/1** SAT/SUN
SEP/OCT
2023

# THE WORLD ALMANAC

**TODAY IN HISTORY**

In 1967, Thurgood Marshall was sworn in as the first Black U.S. Supreme Court justice.

**2**

**MONDAY**
**OCTOBER**
**2023**

Labour Day (Australia—ACT, SA, NSW)
Queen's Birthday (Australia—QLD)

## THE WORLD ALMANAC

### TODAY IN SPORTS HISTORY

In 1951, New York Giants player Bobby Thomson hit the "shot heard 'round the world," a three-run home run in the bottom of the ninth inning to clinch the National League pennant over the Brooklyn Dodgers.

**3** | **TUESDAY**
**OCTOBER**
**2023**

## THE WORLD ALMANAC

**BY THE NUMBERS**

The Statue of Liberty weighs 450,000 pounds, or 225 tons. There are 146 steps from the top of the pedestal (the statue's feet) to the crown platform. The statue's index finger is eight feet long.

**4**

**WEDNESDAY**
**OCTOBER**
**2023**

## THE WORLD ALMANAC

**TODAY IN HISTORY**

In 1947, President Harry S. Truman delivered the first address to be televised from the White House.

**5** | **THURSDAY**
**OCTOBER**
**2023**

## TODAY IN HISTORY

# THE WORLD ALMANAC

More than a decade before the first iPhone was introduced, the first smartphone, IBM's Simon Personal Communicator, went on the market in 1994. A bricklike touchscreen device, it combined a cellular phone with such features as an address book, calendar, calculator, email and faxing capability, and games.

**6**

**FRIDAY**
**OCTOBER**
**2023**

**THIS WEEK IN CELEBRITY BIRTHDAYS:**

**7** ............. Yo-Yo Ma (1955– )

**8** ............. Matt Damon (1970– )

**9** ............. Guillermo del Toro (1964– )

**10** ........... Brett Favre (1969– )

**11** ........... Cardi B (1992– )

**12** ........... Hugh Jackman (1968– )

**13** ........... Sacha Baron Cohen (1971– )

**7/8** SAT/SUN
**OCTOBER**
**2023**

**TODAY IN HISTORY**

In 1888, the Washington Monument opened its interior to visitors for the first time.

**9**

**MONDAY**
**OCTOBER**
**2023**

**TODAY IN SPORTS HISTORY**

In 1964, the opening ceremony of the Olympic Games was held in Tokyo, Japan.

**10**

## THE WORLD ALMANAC

**BY THE NUMBERS**

The count for identified moons in the solar system orbiting planets and dwarf planets stood at 214 as of mid-2020. Several dwarf planet candidates are also known to have moons.

**11** | **WEDNESDAY**
**OCTOBER**
**2023**

**TODAY IN HISTORY**

In 1979, Douglas Adams's *The Hitchhiker's Guide to the Galaxy* was first published in England.

**12**

# THE WORLD ALMANAC

Triskaidekaphobia is a sometimes-mortal fear of or aversion to the number 13. It can also be the basis for a fear of Friday the 13th, sometimes called paraskevidekatriaphobia or friggatriskaidekaphobia.

**13**

**FRIDAY**
**OCTOBER**
**2023**

## THE WORLD ALMANAC

## **THIS WEEK IN CELEBRITY BIRTHDAYS:**

**14** ............ Usher (1978– )

**15** ............ Emeril Lagasse (1959– )

**16** ............ John Mayer (1977– )

**17** ............ Eminem (1972– )

**18** ............ Chuck Berry (1926–2017)

**19** ............ Evander Holyfield (1962– )

**20** ............ Kamala Harris (1964– )

# 14/15

**SAT/SUN**
**OCTOBER**
**2023**

**TODAY IN HISTORY**

In 1923, brothers Roy and Walt Disney founded their "cartoon studio."

**TODAY IN SPORTS HISTORY**

In 1860, the golf tournament that would later become known as the British Open was first held.

# THE WORLD ALMANAC

## BY THE NUMBERS

In 2000, 7.1 percent of light truck vehicles sold in the U.S. were considered cross-utility vehicles. By 2020, cross-utility vehicles accounted for more than half of light truck sales (56.6 percent).

**18**

**WEDNESDAY**
**OCTOBER**
**2023**

**TODAY IN HISTORY**

In 1781, Lord Charles Cornwallis's British troops surrendered at Yorktown, in Virginia, signaling an imminent victory for the Continental Army in the Revolutionary War.

**19**

**THURSDAY
OCTOBER
2023**

**LANGUAGE LESSON**

How to say "hello" in seven languages:

- **Arabic:** Salam
- **Chinese (Mandarin):** Ni hao
- **French:** Bonjour
- **German:** Hallo
- **Hebrew:** Shalom
- **Russian:** Privet (informal)
- **Spanish:** Hola

**20** | **FRIDAY**
**OCTOBER**
**2023**

## THE WORLD ALMANAC

## THIS WEEK IN CELEBRITY BIRTHDAYS:

**21** ............ Carrie Fisher (1956–2016)

**22** ............ Jeff Goldblum (1952– )

**23** ............ Ryan Reynolds (1976– )

**24** ............ Drake (1986– )

**25** ............ Katy Perry (1984– )

**26** ............ Seth MacFarlane (1973– )

**27** ............ Theodore Roosevelt (1858–1919)

**21/22**  SAT/SUN
OCTOBER
2023

**TODAY IN HISTORY**

In 2001, Apple introduced the first iPod, which cost $399 and offered 5 GB of storage.

**23**

MONDAY
OCTOBER
2023

Labour Day (NZ)

**BY THE NUMBERS**

The salary of the president of the United States was last raised on January 20, 2001, to its current annual rate of $400,000.

**24**

United Nations Day

## THE WORLD ALMANAC

**TODAY IN SPORTS HISTORY**

In 1986, the New York Mets came back after a Red Sox error in the tenth inning to beat the Boston Red Sox in Game 6 of the World Series.

**TODAY IN HISTORY**

In 1972, Henry Kissinger, national security advisor to President Richard Nixon, announced "peace is at hand" in Vietnam.

**26**

# THE WORLD ALMANAC

## LANGUAGE LESSON

How to say "yes" in seven languages:

- **Arabic:** naʿam
- **Chinese (Mandarin):** shi [it is so]
- **French:** oui
- **German:** ja
- **Hebrew:** ken
- **Russian:** da
- **Spanish:** sí

**27** | **FRIDAY**
**OCTOBER**
**2023**

**THIS WEEK IN CELEBRITY BIRTHDAYS:**

**10/28** ...... Bill Gates (1955– ); Julia Roberts (1967– )

**10/29** ...... Gabrielle Union (1972– )

**10/30** ...... Henry Winkler (1945– )

**10/31** ...... John Candy (1950–1994)

**11/1** ......... Toni Collette (1972– )

**11/2** ......... David Schwimmer (1966– )

**11/3** ......... Kendall Jenner (1995– )

# 28/29

**SAT/SUN**
**OCTOBER**
**2023**

## THE WORLD ALMANAC

**TODAY IN HISTORY**

In 2005, civil rights pioneer Rosa Parks became the first woman (and third private citizen) to lie in honor in the U.S. Capitol after her death.

**30**

**MONDAY**
**OCTOBER**
**2023**

Bank Holiday (Ireland)

**THE WORLD ALMANAC**

### TODAY IN SPORTS HISTORY

In 1950, Washington Capitols forward Earl Lloyd became the first Black player to appear in an NBA game.

**31**

**TUESDAY
OCTOBER
2023**

Halloween

## THE WORLD ALMANAC

**BY THE NUMBERS**

The U.S. marriage rate dipped during the Depression and peaked sharply just after World War II; the trend after that was more gradual but has fallen in recent years. The U.S. divorce rate generally rose from the 1920s through 1981, when it peaked at 5.3 per 1,000 population, before declining.

**1**

**WEDNESDAY**
**NOVEMBER**
**2023**

## TODAY IN HISTORY

In 1983, President Ronald Reagan signed legislation that made the third Monday of January a federal holiday marking the birth of civil rights leader Martin Luther King Jr.

**2**

**THURSDAY**
**NOVEMBER**
**2023**

## Best American Films of All Time

(According to the American Film Institute)

1. *Citizen Kane* (1941)
2. *The Godfather* (1972)
3. *Casablanca* (1942)
4. *Raging Bull* (1980)
5. *Singin' in the Rain* (1952)

**3**

## THIS WEEK IN CELEBRITY BIRTHDAYS:

**4** ............. Matthew McConaughey (1969– )

**5** ............. Tilda Swinton (1960– )

**6** ............. Emma Stone (1988– )

**7** ............. Lorde (1996– )

**8** ............. Bonnie Raitt (1949– )

**9** ............. Carl Sagan (1934–1996)

**10** ........... Ellen Pompeo (1969– )

# 4/5

SAT/SUN
**NOVEMBER**
**2023**

/Daylight Saving Time ends
(USA, Canada)

## THE WORLD ALMANAC

**TODAY IN HISTORY**

In 1947, *Meet the Press* made its television debut.

**6**

**MONDAY**
**NOVEMBER**
**2023**

**TODAY IN SPORTS HISTORY**

In 1991, L.A. Lakers legend Magic Johnson announced that he had been diagnosed with HIV and would retire from the NBA.

**7**

**TUESDAY**
**NOVEMBER**
**2023**

Election Day (USA)

**BY THE NUMBERS**

The largest tidal ranges (the difference in height between high and low tide) in the world occur in the Bay of Fundy, Canada, where the range of tide reaches 53 feet. The highest tides in the U.S. occur near Anchorage, Alaska, with tidal ranges up to 40 feet.

**8**

WEDNESDAY
**NOVEMBER**
**2023**

## THE WORLD ALMANAC

**TODAY IN HISTORY**

In 1906, Theodore Roosevelt departed for Panama and became the first sitting president to make an official trip outside of the United States.

**9**

**THURSDAY**
**NOVEMBER**
**2023**

**LANGUAGE LESSON**

How to say "please" in seven languages:

- **Arabic:** Men fadlek
- **Chinese (Mandarin):** Qing
- **French:** S'il vous plaît
- **German:** Bitte
- **Hebrew:** Bevakasha
- **Russian:** Pazhalusta
- **Spanish:** Por favor

**10**

## THIS WEEK IN CELEBRITY BIRTHDAYS:

**11** ............ Leonardo DiCaprio (1974– )

**12** ............ Russell Westbrook (1988– )

**13** ............ Whoopi Goldberg (1955– )

**14** ............ Claude Monet (1840–1926)

**15** ............ Karl-Anthony Towns (1995– )

**16** ............ Maggie Gyllenhaal (1977– )

**17** ............ Martin Scorsese (1942– )

# 11/12

**SAT/SUN**
**NOVEMBER**
**2023**

Veterans Day (USA)/
Remembrance Day
(Canada, UK, Ireland, Australia)/
/Diwali
/Remembrance Sunday (UK, Ireland)

**TODAY IN HISTORY**

In 1982, the Vietnam Veterans Memorial was dedicated in Washington, D.C.

**13**

## THE WORLD ALMANAC

### TODAY IN SPORTS HISTORY

In 1956, New York Yankee Mickey Mantle was named American
League MVP for the first time; he finished the season with
52 home runs and 130 RBIs.

**14**

**THE WORLD ALMANAC**

## BY THE NUMBERS

In 2009, the year after its release, Google Chrome held just 3 percent of the web browser market worldwide. By 2021, its share had increased to nearly 70 percent (68.5 percent—down slightly from a high of 71 percent in 2019).

**15**

**WEDNESDAY**
**NOVEMBER**
**2023**

# THE WORLD ALMANAC

**TODAY IN HISTORY**

In 1973, President Richard Nixon signed legislation authorizing the construction of the Trans-Alaska oil pipeline.

**16**

**THURSDAY**
**NOVEMBER**
**2023**

# THE WORLD ALMANAC

### All-Time Highest-Rated U.S. TV Programs

1. *M\*A\*S\*H* final episode (1983)
2. *Dallas* "Who Shot J.R.?" episode (1980)
3. *Roots* part 8 (1977)
4. Super Bowl XVI (1982)
5. Super Bowl XVII (1983)

**17**

**FRIDAY**
**NOVEMBER**
**2023**

## THIS WEEK IN CELEBRITY BIRTHDAYS:

**18** ............ Owen Wilson (1968– )

**19** ............ Adam Driver (1983– )

**20** ............ Joe Biden (1942– )

**21** ............ Goldie Hawn (1945– )

**22** ............ Scarlett Johansson (1984– )

**23** ............ Miley Cyrus (1992– )

**24** ............ Colin Hanks (1977– )

# 18/19

**SAT/SUN**
**NOVEMBER**
**2023**

**THE WORLD ALMANAC**

### TODAY IN HISTORY

In 1985, operating system Microsoft Windows 1.0 was shipped to stores.

**20**

**MONDAY**
**NOVEMBER**
**2023**

**THE WORLD ALMANAC**

### TODAY IN SPORTS HISTORY

In 1942, the NHL discontinued overtime in regular-season games because of wartime restrictions on train schedules. Overtime was not restored until 1983.

**21**

**TUESDAY**
**NOVEMBER**
**2023**

# THE WORLD ALMANAC

## BY THE NUMBERS

In 2021, 56.6 percent of the world's population lived in an urban area. That proportion is expected to increase to an estimated 62.5 percent in 2035.

**22** | **WEDNESDAY**
**NOVEMBER**
**2023**

# THE WORLD ALMANAC

**TODAY IN HISTORY**

In 1936, the first issue of *Life* magazine was published (as relaunched under *Time* publisher Henry Luce).

## THE WORLD ALMANAC

**LANGUAGE LESSON**

How to say "thank you very much" in seven languages:

- **Arabic:** Shokran jazeelan
- **Chinese (Mandarin):** Xie xie
- **French:** Merci beaucoup
- **German:** Danke schön
- **Hebrew:** Toda raba
- **Russian:** Spasiba
- **Spanish:** Muchas gracias

## 24

**FRIDAY**
**NOVEMBER**
**2023**

**THIS WEEK IN CELEBRITY BIRTHDAYS:**

**11/25** ...... Christina Applegate (1971– )

**11/26** ...... DJ Khaled (1975– )

**11/27** ...... Jimi Hendrix (1942–1970)

**11/28** ...... Jon Stewart (1962– )

**11/29** ...... Anna Faris (1976– )

**11/30** ...... Chrissy Teigen (1985– )

**12/1** ........ Zoë Kravitz (1988– )

# 25/26

**SAT/SUN**
**NOVEMBER**
**2023**

# THE WORLD ALMANAC

## TODAY IN HISTORY

In 1895, Alfred Nobel signed his last will and testament, establishing the Nobel Prize.

**27**

**MONDAY
NOVEMBER
2023**

## TODAY IN SPORTS HISTORY

In 1979, Billy Smith of the New York Islanders became the first goalie in NHL history to be credited with a goal. After an opposing player mistakenly hit the puck into his own team's net, Smith was awarded the goal as the last Islander to touch the puck.

**28** | **TUESDAY**
**NOVEMBER**
**2023**

**BY THE NUMBERS**

Between 1901 and 2021, the Nobel Prizes (and the prize in economic sciences) were awarded 609 times to 975 people and organizations. The youngest winner, Malala Yousafzai, was just 17 years old; the oldest winner, John B. Goodenough, was 97 years old.

**29**

WEDNESDAY
**NOVEMBER**
2023

## THE WORLD ALMANAC

**TODAY IN HISTORY**

In 2004, Ken Jennings's record 74-game winning streak on the TV game show *Jeopardy!* came to an end.

## 30

**THURSDAY**
**NOVEMBER**
**2023**

St. Andrew's Day (UK)

**Longest Running Broadway Shows of All-Time**

(by number of performances as of September 2021)

1. *Phantom of the Opera* (1988– )
2. *Chicago* revival (1996– )
3. *The Lion King* (1987– )
4. *Cats* (1982–2000)
5. *Wicked* (2003– )

**1**

FRIDAY
**DECEMBER**
2023

# THE WORLD ALMANAC

## THIS WEEK IN CELEBRITY BIRTHDAYS:

**2** .............. Britney Spears (1981– )

**3** .............. Julianne Moore (1960– )

**4** .............. Jay-Z (1969– )

**5** .............. Walt Disney (1901–1966)

**6** .............. Giannis Antetokounmpo (1994– )

**7** .............. Yuzuru Hanyu (1994– )

**8** .............. Nicki Minaj (1982– )

# 2/3

**SAT/SUN**
**DECEMBER**
**2023**

**TODAY IN HISTORY**

In 1956, the so-called Million-Dollar Quartet—Johnny Cash, Jerry Lee Lewis, Carl Perkins, and Elvis Presley—played their first and only session together at Sun Studios in Memphis, Tennessee.

**4**

MONDAY
**DECEMBER**
**2023**

## THE WORLD ALMANAC

**TODAY IN SPORTS HISTORY**

In 1947, Joe Louis beat Jersey Joe Walcott in a split decision to retain the heavyweight title.

**5**

**TUESDAY**
**DECEMBER**
**2023**

## THE WORLD ALMANAC

### BY THE NUMBERS

The lowest temperature ever recorded in Antarctica was −128.6°F, on July 21, 1983. This is nearly 120 degrees colder than the Australian continental record of −9.4°F, set on June 29, 1994.

**6**

**TODAY IN HISTORY**

In 1941, Japan launched a surprise attack on Pearl Harbor, Hawaii.

**7**

**THURSDAY**
**DECEMBER**
**2023**

Hanukkah (begins at sundown)

## Top-Selling Albums of All Time
### (as of 2021)

1. *Their Greatest Hits (1971–1975)*, Eagles
2. *Thriller*, Michael Jackson
3. *Hotel California*, Eagles
4. *Back in Black*, AC/DC
5. *The Beatles*, The Beatles

**8**

## THIS WEEK IN CELEBRITY BIRTHDAYS:

**9** .............. Simon Helberg (1980– )

**10** ............ Emily Dickinson (1830–1886)

**11** ............ Hailee Steinfeld (1996– )

**12** ............ Frank Sinatra (1915–1998)

**13** ............ Taylor Swift (1989– )

**14** ............ Vanessa Hudgens (1988– )

**15** ............ Don Johnson (1949– )

**9/10**

SAT/SUN
**DECEMBER**
**2023**

/Human Rights Day

# THE WORLD ALMANAC

**TODAY IN HISTORY**

In 2008, investment banker Bernie Madoff was arrested for perpetrating one of the largest Ponzi scheme–style frauds in U.S. history.

**11**

**THE WORLD ALMANAC**

### TODAY IN SPORTS HISTORY

In 1930, MLB's rules committee issued a revised code. Among many other changes, balls that bounce into the stands were to be ruled automatic doubles, rather than home runs.

**12**

# THE WORLD ALMANAC

**BY THE NUMBERS**

The U.S. video game industry generated $56.91 billion in revenue in 2020: $7.92 billion on hardware, including peripherals, and $49 billion on software, including in-game purchases and subscriptions. Spending was up 27 percent from $44.93 billion in 2019.

**13**

## THE WORLD ALMANAC

**TODAY IN HISTORY**

In 1799, former President George Washington died at Mount Vernon, his home in Virginia.

**14**

**THURSDAY**
**DECEMBER**
**2023**

# THE WORLD ALMANAC

The original Purple Heart, designated as the Badge of Military Merit, was established by General George Washington on August 7, 1782. Following the American Revolution, the honor fell into disuse until 1932, the 200th anniversary of Washington's birth.

**15**

FRIDAY
**DECEMBER**
2023

Hanukkah ends

# THE WORLD ALMANAC

## THIS WEEK IN CELEBRITY BIRTHDAYS:

**16** ............ Benjamin Bratt (1963– )

**17** ............ Sarah Paulson (1974– )

**18** ........... Billie Eilish (2001– )

**19** ........... Jake Gyllenhaal (1980– )

**20** ........... Jonah Hill (1983– )

**21** ........... Samuel L. Jackson (1948– )

**22** ........... Ralph Fiennes (1962– )

## 16/17

**SAT/SUN**
**DECEMBER**
**2023**

**THE WORLD ALMANAC**

**TODAY IN HISTORY**

In 1892, Pyotr Ilyich Tchaikovsky's ballet *The Nutcracker* premiered in St. Petersburg, Russia.

**18**

**THE WORLD ALMANAC**

**TODAY IN SPORTS HISTORY**

In 1980, Brigham Young University's football team, down 20 points with just under four minutes to play, staged a comeback to defeat Southern Methodist University in the Holiday Bowl, 46–45.

**19**

### THE WORLD ALMANAC

**BY THE NUMBERS**

As of 2019, there were 9,057 public libraries in the United States, welcoming an estimated 1.243 billion visitors per year.

**20**

WEDNESDAY
**DECEMBER**
2023

## THE WORLD ALMANAC

**TODAY IN HISTORY**

In 1913, the *New York World* newspaper published Arthur Wynne's first "word-cross"—considered by many to be the first modern crossword puzzle.

**21**

## The World Almanac

### World's Most Visited Amusement Parks
(2019)

1. Magic Kingdom, Walt Disney World, Lake Buena Vista, Florida, 20.96 million visitors

2. Disneyland, Anaheim, California, 18.67 million visitors

3. Tokyo Disneyland, Tokyo, Japan, 17.91 million visitors

4. Tokyo DisneySea, Tokyo, Japan, 14.65 million visitors

5. Universal Studios Japan, Osaka, Japan, 14.50 million visitors

**22** | **FRIDAY**
**DECEMBER**
**2023**

Winter Solstice

# THE WORLD ALMANAC

## THIS WEEK IN CELEBRITY BIRTHDAYS:

**23** ............ Eddie Vedder (1964– )

**24** ............ Ryan Seacrest (1974– )

**25** ............ Humphrey Bogart (1899–1957)

**26** ............ Kit Harington (1986– )

**27** ............ Timothée Chalamet (1995– )

**28** ............ John Legend (1978– )

**29** ............ Alison Brie (1982– )

## 23/24

**SAT/SUN**
**DECEMBER**
**2023**

/Christmas Eve

**TODAY IN HISTORY**

In 1990, the first web server, web browser, and website went live on the computer of Tim Berners-Lee, inventor of the World Wide Web.

# 25

**MONDAY**
**DECEMBER**
**2023**

Christmas Day

**TODAY IN SPORTS HISTORY**

In 1908, boxer Jack Johnson defeated Tommy Burns, becoming the first Black heavyweight champion.

**26**

Kwanzaa begins (USA)
Boxing Day
(Canada, NZ, UK, Australia—except SA)
St. Stephen's Day (Ireland)
Proclamation Day (Australia—SA)

# THE WORLD ALMANAC

### BY THE NUMBERS

Of refuse collected as so-called municipal solid waste in the U.S. in 2018, paper represented 23.1%; food 21.6%; plastics 12.2%; yard trimmings 12.1%; rubber, leather, and textiles 8.9%; metals 8.8%; wood 6.2%; glass 4.2%; and other material 2.9%. About 32.1% of the refuse was recycled or composted.

**27**

WEDNESDAY
**DECEMBER**
2023

**TODAY IN HISTORY**

In 1973, President Richard Nixon signed the Endangered Species Act.

## LANGUAGE LESSON

How to say "goodbye" in seven languages:

- **Arabic:** Ma'a salama
- **Chinese (Mandarin):** Zai jian
- **French:** Au revoir
- **German:** Auf wiedersehen
- **Hebrew:** Lehitraot
- **Russian:** Da svidan'ya
- **Spanish:** Adiós

**29**

**FRIDAY**
**DECEMBER**
**2023**

# THE WORLD ALMANAC

## THIS WEEK IN CELEBRITY BIRTHDAYS:

**12/30**...... Tiger Woods (1975– )

**12/31** ...... Diane von Fürstenberg (1946– )

**1/1**........... Grandmaster Flash (1958– )

**1/2** .......... Isaac Asimov (1920–1992)

**1/3** .......... Michael Schumacher (1969– )

**1/4** .......... Kris Bryant (1992– )

**1/5** .......... Bradley Cooper (1975– )

# 30/31

SAT/SUN
**DECEMBER**
2023

www.andrewsmcmeel.com

ISBN: 978-1-5248-7318-9

Start dates for the seasons of the year are presented in Universal Time.

Every effort has been made to ensure the accuracy of listed holiday dates; however, some may have changed after publication for official or cultural reasons.

www.andrewsmcmeel.com